MW00849148

SONNETS FOR AN OLD CENTURY

José Rivera

BROADWAY PLAY PUBLISHING INC
224 E 62nd St, NY NY 10065-8201
212 772-8334 fax: 212 772-8358
BroadwayPlayPub.com

SONNETS FOR AN OLD CENTURY
© Copyright 2004 by José Rivera

All rights reserved. This work is fully protected under the copyright laws of the United States of America. No part of this publication may be photocopied, reproduced, stored in a retrieval system, or transmitted, in any form or by any means, electronic, mechanical, recording, or otherwise, without the prior permission of the publisher. Additional copies of this play are available from the publisher.

Written permission is required for live performance of any sort. This includes readings, cuttings, scenes, and excerpts. For amateur and stock performances, please contact Broadway Play Publishing Inc. For all other rights also please contact the author c/o B P P I.

First printing: October 2004
Second printing: June 2014

I S B N: 978-0-88145-252-5

Book design: Marie Donovan
Typeface: Palatino
Printed and bound in the U S A

SONNETS FOR AN OLD CENTURY was developed by the Relentless Theater Company, New York Theater Workshop, The Mark Taper Forum, The Philadelphia Theater Company, The La Jolla Playhouse, Ensemble Studio Theater West, and CalArts.

SONNETS FOR AN OLD CENTURY received its world premiere production at the Greeway Arts Alliance (Pierson Blaetz and Whitney Weston, Co-Artistic Directors) in Los Angeles on 14 January 2000. Oscar Arguello, Laura Frank and Maricela Ochoa were co-producers. The cast and creative contributors were:

Antoinette Abbamonte	Lesa Carlson
Andrew Carrillo	Gary Carter
Juan Carlos Cisneros	Lynn Dandridge
James DiStefano	Mark Ferreira
Valentina Ferreira	Gretchen German
Billy Kane	Newton Kaneshiro
Kevin Kelly	Wendy Johnson
Diana C Larios	Javi Mulero
Masashi Odate	Rosana Potter
Reiko	René Rivera
Steven Ruge	Michael Teisan
Kiersten Van Horne	Whitney Weston

Direction & design . . . . .James Eric
Scenic art . . . . Gabriel Dell Jr
Lighting design . . . . Cheryl Waters
Costume design . . . . .Naomi Yoshida-Rodriguez
Stage manager . . . . Irma Escamilla

SPECIAL THANKS

Juliette Carillo, Olivia Honneger, John Ortiz, Michi Barall, Geno Silva, Yusef Bulos, Alene Dawson, Sam Wellington, John Socas, Laura Tishler, Damian Young, Yancy Arias, Marin Hinkle, Susan Knight, Jaime Sanchez, Irma St Paul, Daphne Rubin-Vega, Kevin Carroll, Jojo Gonzales, Ching Valdez-Aran, Chris McCann, Jonathan Lisecki, Felicity Jones, Jessica Hecht, Jaye Austin-Williams, Missy Pyle, Gary Perez, Stephanie Berry, Rob Campbell, Larry Ash, Brian Dinges, Ben Hammer, Kathleen Wallace, Rachel Malkenhorst, Jesse Borrego, Richard Coca, Dawn Saito, Alex Fernandez, Tom Lenoci, Michael Manual, Marissa Chibas, Tony Abatemarco, John Vargas, Natalie Griffiths, Melody Butiu, Camilla Sanes, Moisés Kaufman, Kevin Jackosn, Corey Madden, Lisa Peterson, Neel Keller, Elizabeth Bennett, Michael Greif, Christine Jones, and Julia Edwards.

(i who have died am alive again today,
and this is the sun's birthday; this is the birth
day of life and of love and wings: and of the gay
great happening illimitably earth)

e e cummings

i thank you god

ACT ONE

(The sonnets can be performed in any order. Feel free to do as many or as few as you wish.)

(The space could be a tunnel, a cave, a warehouse, an airplane hangar, catacombs, or a seedy office building with ugly fluorescent lighting—but it's a large space.)

(The many people who appear in the space are from various parts of the United States. There are Latinos, blacks, Asians, whites. There are gays and straights, children and old people. All are strangers to each other.)

WENDY JOHNSON

(To the group)

You stand here and make your statement.

That's it.
You want to fight with existence?
Go for it. You want to scream?
Knock yourself out.

Just remember:
your words go out to the universe,
all your words, to be, I don't know,
recycled among the living—like
rain, like part of—
some ecology of the spirit.

It's the last and only time you have
to give your side of the story, as
far as I know.

JAVI MULERO

We would eat liverwurst on black bread
with mustard and onions and have sex.

We would have sex on tattered, sticky
pages of the Sunday *New York Times*.

We would have sex after walking
across the Brooklyn Bridge, cold
October afternoons, staying home from
work, angry at our office jobs among
the walking dead and art wannabees.

We would have sex instead of air.

We would have sex while burning
garbage fell on our fire escape
because the maniac on the floor above
us decided devils were living in his trash.

We would have sex while water dripped
through our ceiling because
the maniac on the floor above
us kept the water in his bathtub running while he
went off to visit a brother on Staten
Island who had communicated with
devils and had salient advise on how
to use them for your own benefit.

We would have sex while the maniac on
the floor above us returned from
Staten Island, fell in the hallway,
and pounded the floor with his fists.

We would have sex after visiting the
maniac on the floor above us, his
eyes black and blue, his shirt
saturated with blood, who told us he
was beaten by a gang in Red Hook who
he tried to buy drugs from on his way
to visit his brother in Staten Island.

We had sex after explaining to the
maniac on the floor above us that Red
Hook isn't on the way to Staten
Island and we had to get the super to
turn off the water in his tub and the
super is going to recommend that the
maniac on the floor above us, who
sees devils living in many corners of
his life, be evicted immediately for
nonpayment of rent and for constantly
coming home from Red Hook bleeding
from the face.

We had sex after an attempted
assassination of the
President of the United States.

We would have sex after returning
from Westchester where her parents
lived and inspired tears and had the
power to reduce her to the status of
an undisciplined punk with no respect
for their values and customs, who had
sex out of wedlock with a Puerto
Rican, in many locations and quite frequently.

We would have sex without protection.

We would have sex while children
starved, racists ran for office, war
was waged on the poor, exotic and
never-to-be-duplicated forms of life

were deleted, fundamentalists
dictated the terms of our living, the
hoarding classes perfected devious
and more efficient ways to horde and
the country drowned in capital,
optimism, envy, and bullshit.

We would have sex when we didn't feel like it.

We would have sex after bad dreams.

We would have sex after burying our
parents and grandparents, while work
became more and more meaningless, and
friends questioned their marriages.

We would have sex while our children asked about sex.

We would have sex in spasms, in
waves, in circles, in small
violences, in secret ecstasies, in
patient waiting, in doubts, in
forgotten languages, in extreme
loneliness, in promises kept, in
wishes left unacknowledged, in ritual
fantasy—in peril and in peace.

CAMILIA SANES

I was known as quiet and studious.

My glasses embarrassed me
and I hid them often
and suffered the anger of my mother
who also wore glasses,
but she was proud of hers.

She was studious too.
She covered the house in books.
She read in the bathtub

and read to me every night of my life.
Long great hard books full of characters
and interweaving chapters
and sentences with so many commas and colors.
Friendly books with heroes.

I listened so hard.
I settled into my bed
trying to melt into the sheets,
trying to surround my body
with the warm mattress.
I don't think I really heard the words.
I didn't need to.

The words were like waves on the beach,
lifting me softly,
tumbling me in crazy rapids,
pushing me under for moments
of brief, airless, gasping terror,
then delivering me up again—
up to air,
up to sunlight,
up to the light in my small bedroom
and my mother's shape on the bed,
her out-of-style glasses
glistening with mischief and hard work.

The words washed away
the stress of nasty girls
who excluded me on the playground.
The words washed away
the tests that I hated and failed,
despite my glasses and my studying.

The words were invisible fingers
my mother employed
to hold me close and warm,
to squeeze my brain a little tighter,
to hold in firm embrace

my throbbing lungs,
my mighty muscled heart.

She was a dreamer.
She dreamed worlds and they appeared
next to the bathtub in hardcover.

Sometimes I didn't know
if I was really there.
Sometimes I wondered
if maybe she dreamed me too.
She needed a little daughter
who looked and acted like she did
and she forced me by incredible
willpower through the fallopian tubes
of her mind
and squeezed me out of her imagination,
blue and bawling,
complete with glasses and gratitude,
asleep at her side in our cozy bed,
dreamer and dream together.

ANNE O'SULLIVAN

Um.
Let's see.
I learned a few things while I was there...
over there...
wherever there is.
Was.
Is that what I should talk about?
I don't know if I can talk about no sex.

Okay.
What I learned.
Um.
Children?

Children contain all the necessary
wisdom to create a civilization.

Um.
Evil is unexplainable.
So don't even try.
If you suddenly don't understand
the words and actions of your family
members or best friends, think drugs.
Money fucks relationships.
That one's obvious.
All straight men want to fuck
all straight women all the time.
Rice and beans are better than potatoes.

You will never be able to fully
forgive your parents.
Dreams are the Earth's telepathy.
Eat as much as you can, a famine is
coming. Baby boomers have completely
run out of Great Ideas.
Strong moonlight is healing.
Let people know when you're in love
with them. Lies make your lips smaller.
Pay bills a day late.
Strangers are opportunities for mischief—
take advantage.

Paint a classroom.
Wash all your dishes by hand
and contemplate the value of water.
Sins are man-made.
Never trivialize the Supreme Being.
Good prayer is biofeedback.
You can't love a child too much.
Don't fuck with people who believe in you.
Anger is contagious,
so be careful who you sleep with.
Rice and beans are better than pasta.

Grow one edible fruit or vegetable
to supplement your income.
Baseball is a game not a metaphor.
Life is neither a dream nor a cabaret.
You don't have to choose between
passion and security.
There are many parallel Americas
and the rich have the better one.
Listen to your jealousy.
I was shot in the head and I think,
to satisfy the Second Amendment,
all Americans should own one Eighteenth Century
musket and that's it.
Religion and spirituality are two
completely different things in America.

DAWNN LEWIS

Night of the unrest,
I was at a screening in Santa Monica.
The week before,
the radio was stolen out of my car.
At the screening, there's no T V,
nobody really knows what's up.
I leave the screening around eleven,
with no idea what's happening,
except I knew the verdict came down
and I'm feeling real sick to my stomach at this point.
And I'm driving back to Pasadena on the 10...
and I see this black towering mass
on the freeway right in front of me,
a huge, black funnel, like, I'm not shittin' you,
someone just let some evil genie out of a bottle,
and I'm all, "Fuck me, it's a tornado!
There's a fucking tornado in L A!"
And I'm freaking out!

Then I see *another* one, next to it, *another* one.
Then I realize: no; that's smoke; the city's on fire;
and then I see it's only burning
on my *right, south* of the 10,
in the black part of town.
And when I understand this...
I feel those tornadoes lifting up my car
and spinning me in space and
I'm part of this terrifying wind
blowing all our hopes away:
the firestorm in the neighborhood
full of old hatreds,
left over anxiety from the Watts riots,
years of blame and disappointment,
swirling all together in a huge funnel of air,
black and thick, taking me to some anti-Oz
where the yellow brick road's red with blood
and tornadoes don't stop spinning,
and they spin continuously,
to this day, to this minute,
and all I want to do is spin around,
throwing curses and venom in every direction,
at everyone who's forgotten...

RICK COCA

I was waiting outside the house
for almost an hour.
My *novia* was working in this house.
Anglo family.
Watching their children.
They were supposed to get back by eleven-thirty.

It was past midnight.
We didn't think they'd want me in their house
so I waited in the car on the street in front.

I drove a small and dented Toyota.
The neighborhood was rich.
Big houses, not too much happening at night.
Dead and dark.
Sometimes you see coyotes looking for food.
Or an opossum crawling across the road.
They are very slow animals.
No wonder so many of them die.
You see their guts spattering all over the road.
They are not pretending then.

Animals fascinate me.
Where I grew up you lived with animals.
You understood their habits.
You paid attention to what they needed
or they would die.
If they die, you die.
I watched them being born!
I got used to blood and birth.
I understood the great variety of shit
in the animal kingdom.

My mother taught me to kill chickens
with my hands.
You grab them around the neck and then
you spin them around.
They struggle and some of them
can really cut you bad if you're not careful.
When I was a child I loved to kill them like that.

Later I butchered pigs.
I pretended the pig was a condemned man,
a murderer, rapist, with no soul,
who never repented,
and spit at the priest giving him Last Rites
and mocked the sacraments
and the family of the victim,
boasted he raped little girls.
I held the knife tight.

Looked at the struggling, confused pig.
Imagined the rapist or the unrepentant murderer
and I was chosen by the court to execute this scum.
I never smiled.
I never let the pig's—
I mean the prisoner's—
screams distract me.
I plunged the knife into its soft throat—
far as it could go—
and I cut and cut and the animal screamed
like a man and I imagined
the bleeding prisoner
finally understanding the meaning of his crimes,
repenting, fearing God,
believing in God's wisdom,
God's punishment, which I carried out.
I was the messenger of God,
the word of God, I said,
"don't kill," "don't rape," "don't sin,"...
I was the terrible messenger
and this knife was my message.
I took myself very seriously
when I was ten years old.

I feared nothing except goats.
I wouldn't kill goats.
I wouldn't come near them.
They have haunted eyes, God protect me!
They seem like the reincarnated souls
of madmen.
When they cry out, it sounds like your name.
I would practically shit myself in fear.
I begged my father to get rid of the goats.

One day—I cried in front of my father
and he was so offended
he hit me over the head
with the handle of a machete

and told me to stop acting like a girl.
He locked me in the goats' pen
for a day to punish me
and those madmen brayed
and shouted at me,
told me their stories,
their past lives.
It was hard to make out their words.
But I understood enough.

One had set his hair on fire.
One had eaten rats.
One believed he was Pope John XXIII.
One had sat in a room twelve years,
sitting in his own shit,
dreaming of space travel.

I screamed at them to stop talking to me.
Worried, my father let me out at dinner time—
he was going to make me spend the night there,
but changed his mind,
afraid a night with those madmen
would drive me so insane everyone would pity him
for having an insane child in his family—
and my father hated people's pity
more than he hated having a sissy son.
I wiped my eyes and walked out the pen.
I never cried in front of him again.

To this day, animals fail to move me
with their dying, their breeding—so what?
The coyotes hurrying through these
bigshot Anglo neighborhoods at night,
ignoring me in my Toyota
as I wait for my girlfriend—so what?

I waited out there nearly an hour.
I was low in my seat,
thinking of my youth in Nicaragua
among animals.

It was dark and quiet.
I was about to fall asleep.
Far away I heard a car.
It wasn't going fast.
I thought "no."

I didn't move.
I could feel the sweat in my hands.
My asshole tightening.
The car had very bright headlights
and it stopped right behind me,
engine running,
lights shining into my car,
I thought "no."
I waited and decided to sit up.
The police lights shot on,
red and blue swirls colliding in my face,
my stomach turning into boiling water,
my mouth dry.
Two men got out.
One of them shined a flashlight in my face.
I waited.
The other cop stood behind the first
and he waited.
Man's eyes were cold.
Man's eyes stared right into me.
I turned my head
and wouldn't look in his eyes
as the other one told me
to get out of the car very, very slow,
hand on his gun,
the night very still,
coyotes long gone,
scared away by the action, instinctual.
I stood there
and explained what my business was
on this street
and one of the cops looked at me

the way I used to look at the pigs
I was about to slaughter,
cold, convinced of my higher duty,
the spokesman of God,
the messenger,
the punisher,
the death-bringer.

MARICELA OCHOA

I wanted to be a ballerina or an astronaut.

In my imagination, day after day,
I practiced dancing on the moon.
If there was life on Mars, I would waltz with it.
Before the accident, I kept a journal.
I drew pictures of other Life Forms.
Creatures with sticky tentacles and multiple eyes—
I drew rock monsters, worms with intelligence,
plasma jellies with attitude—
and all of them had rhythm.
They could salsa!
They could tango!
They could do splits!

I learned that dancing on Jupiter is a challenge.
Heavy gas, lots of gravity—
good for slow dancing.
But you can't jitterbug there.
Before I was paralyzed,
my body could do almost anything.
I learned movements instantly.
My body was a library of dance styles.
On long interplanetary voyages
I imagined leading the crew in the Charleston,
the minuet, the merengue, the hula,
and the mashed potato.

Wars between rival civilizations
in the dark corners of space
would be averted
because my body
would translate between species—
and one-eyed creatures of one world
would read the words
of ten-armed creatures of another world
by following the movements of my hips.

My legs would speak of peace.
My torso would convince
skeptical generals of warlike peoples
that love is a greater conqueror than conquest.
My body would be a peace treaty.
My limbs would be paragraphs on disarmament.
My eyes would be the signatures
of diverse universal leaders.
And my toes would be the footnotes.

MICHI BARALL

I have so many questions, I don't know where to begin.
Let's start with the research I was doing. So is it true?
About the river of galaxies? I have to know this!

The expanding universe—okay?—expands uniformly
in all directions according to the Big Bang theory.
But then we discovered that the expanding universe
wasn't so uniform after all. That, in fact, there is a river
of galaxies heading off in the direction of Virgo—a
massive flow of galaxies being sucked into *one direction*,
completely at odds with the Big Bang theory. All over
the scientific community people were freaking out.

Then a few years ago, my colleagues and I—we called
ourselves the Seven Samurai—we discovered that a
Massive Great Attractor is pulling a quarter of the known

universe—a two hundred million light year region of space—at the speed of one-point-two million miles per hour. *Pulling it.*

Why? What's out there? Are they giving away immortality? Is it something really bright and shiny? Is it something musical? An astronomical Pied Piper hauling a quarter of the universe's known mass in one direction? I mean, how good can it be? Or is it something sinister? Is something out there eating matter? Is the universe flat? Should we fear, like the sailors of antiquity, the horizon—because there's a point beyond which we can't go? A falling off point? I gotta know this!

I had a thing happen to me; I was eight. I was in my backyard. Alone. My mother was upstairs taking a nap because the baby was finally asleep. I was playing with a sword stabbing invisible enemies.

Then the light around me changed. I dropped the sword, looked around. And something on the other side of the yard was...calling me—*pulling me*—to it. I don't remember well! It was a light, it was a sound like music, it was warm, it was friendly, but very stern, it was large, it was very strong, and I could feel my body *leaning* that way. I looked down, and the grass, too, was leaning that way. The air seemed to be blowing in that one direction. I took a step toward this thing, this Attraction. I noticed my soccer ball rolling toward it. Getting faster the further it got from me. I wanted to cry. Each step, it felt a little stronger, it seemed to get a little brighter. I was starting to fight it, breathing very hard, I could hear myself crying, really crying hard. I noticed all the trees were bending in that direction too as if they were pointing something out to me. I called my mother's name! It was like the sound of my voice was suddenly grabbed by big hands and thrown to the other side of the yard. I saw a few of my tears leave my face and go right into the swirling eye of this Big Attraction. There was no sound but the soft music and my hard crying.

Then it stopped. The whole thing just stopped. The music, the lights, gone.

Whatever it was, had it gotten what it wanted? Did it just want a couple of my tears? The sound of my voice as I called my mother?

All my life, I've been attracted to stars and night skies, trying to understand what happened to me when I was eight: hoping, with the aid of telescopes and satellites, to hear that eerie music again and feel that warmth. I still don't know if the thing wanted to eat me or love me. I was attracted to the big dome of the Planetarium— but then the shaking started and the whole structure, attracted by gravity, collapsed on me and sent me here. Attracted to the Big Questions of the universe, I think of that river of galaxies, wondering if it's pulled by the same force that nearly seduced me in my backyard, desperately needing to know if it will eat us or love us.

JOHN ORTIZ

Last year we were in Puerto Rico.
And we were on the beach.
Sun going down.
Beautiful, red, bursting sun, dropping...
golden coins into the ocean.
And I was eating a mango.
And it was sticky and sweet.
And Therese was rubbing my back,
real gentle, and sometimes her hand
would come down to my ass.
And someone on the beach
was playing a twelve-string mandolin

and a little girl was singing
in a high stratosphere voice,
pure and brown like her skin...
these golden flecks around her greenish eyes...
like she'd been kissed there
by the sun's miniature lips...
little kiss-tattoos
around the solar system of her mulatto eyes:
her voice bathing me in warm, fat notes,
ancient notes full of slavery and passion.
And I asked myself as I stood there on the beach:
why am I not happy here?
Why don't I stay here and live like this
the rest of my life?
Why, God, isn't this enough?
And I realize now—my ambition
was like a disease in my system.
This disease was commanding me
to leave paradise and kill myself
with work twenty-four hours a day.
And even if this disease destroyed me,
I had to obey it.
It would not let me go
no matter how much I drown it
in mangoes and music and sunshowers.

ESTHER SCOTT

I ran for President.
No one knew me.
All my life I wanted to be President.
The apex of my life!

I went door-to-door
trying to get enough signatures
to put me on the ballot in Michigan.
Most people slammed their doors in my face.

I never got any media coverage.
But I gathered signatures.
I had a few passionate followers.

I had a message: in 1990, thirteen percent of all voters
were from families whose incomes were under fifteen
thousand dollars.

In 1992 that percentage had dropped to eleven percent.

In 1994, of all the families making less than fifteen
thousand dollars a year, only seven-point-seven percent
bothered to vote.

In 1989 the inequality of wealth distribution in the
United States was at a sixty year high.

Imagine what it is now!

The top one percent of families ranked by financial
wealth had forty-eight percent of all the wealth in the
country.

The top twenty percent owned ninety-four percent of
the country's wealth.

In 1989, thirty-five percent of all families of color
reported zero or negative net worth.

So I got a few hundred signatures.
I shook a few hundred hands.
In brief moments I made real connection
to real people.
I gave them a little hope.
I made their country a little better for them.
For a couple of minutes there were
a few people who could smell change in the air.
Who witnessed the unlikely birth of a new nation.
I ate a lot of red meat with the people.
Funny.
I couldn't tell if they were humoring me or not.
But I drank a few cold beers.

SAM WELLINGTON

I'm surrounded by strangers.
I'm trying to just deal.
I want answers.
I'd like to see the man in charge.
I'd like to see a schedule!
I'd like to know when I get to set the pace of events
around here!

I operated a forklift.
And I had my problems with substance abuse.
Okay?
But that's all past now.
That shit's gone bye-bye as far as I'm concerned.
As far as I know doing hard drugs
isn't technically a sin in the record books
of any organized religion I'm aware of.
Last time I checked.

I partied.
Sure, I partied.
I liked to kickback, shoot the shit
with a few friends over a barbecue grill,
Coors Light in one hand, spatula in the other.
Entertain the masses.
I'd drink far more than my share.
I'd get pissed—
been known to happen.
Get a little mellow—
girls look exceptionally good, why not?
Last time I perused the holy pages,
I don't believe beer or pussy
were on the list of frowned-upon human activities.
I can say pussy if I want!

Consenting adults, of course,
I didn't chase no children,
didn't offer beer or pot to minors.
If I ended up in the arms of a married woman,
I know I wasn't breaching any kind of
earth-shattering moral responsibility.
As long as I wasn't coveting her.
I wasn't *coveting* her, I was *copulating* her.
And I didn't go for sodomy!
So you can't fault me on that line of reasoning.
And it's not like I'm some kind of Samson of the
love-crowd:
my success rate's pretty single digits most times.
Usually it was drink, drink—puke, puke—crawl on
hands and knees over cold tile—wish to God I owned
a handgun so I could nullify the drumbeat in the
whimpering bloodpools of my brain.
Thoughts of self-slaughter,
even if you read the fine
print under this heading,
isn't the actual event and
therefore not covered in this clause!

Never killed no one.
Never worshipped graven images.
Never had no pictures of Baal or Mithra or Mothra or
whatever those Babylonian deities were called.
Didn't worship no cows either!
Except a couple of human ones!
Never bought Proctor and Gamble Satanic products.
I've broken the law.
Sure.
Flat broke so bad, one year, had to steal medicines
when I got sick—
especially my asthma and those
inhalers are marked up to extremes,
talk about sin.
So I'd lift a few of those.

Yeah, that's theft, that's stealing,
that's, that's pretty certain,
you know, no-holds-barred sinning.
You got me there.

I remember from the Bible classes,
they'd have a drawing of a quart of
milk and that's your pure, white soul.
But the sinners have little black
smudges on their quarts of milk.
And anything other than actual white
milk in that bottle was fucked.
It ruined the perfection.
And it pretty much ruined your
chances of experiencing the bliss
of Heavenly reunion with the Great Creator—
though I gotta say I'm still waiting
for the bliss part to kick in here.
So I guess my thieveries are showing
up on the outer-lining of my soul.
But I'll tell you how unfair that is.
I was hungry, I was having asthma attacks.
I was not greedy.
And I wasn't packing anything.

And, you know, these were Man's laws
I was breaking and I really do think
something as small and temporary
as Man's laws have no real long-term
effect on something as total and
permanent as the human soul.
That's just my opinion.
The opinion of a working man.
I know I can look right into the
terrible eyes of our Lord Jesus
and be secure in the knowledge that the
smudges on my eternal soul are slight
and unimportant and simply the wages

of living in an imperfect world run by
man and his laughable laws.
Looks like I covered most of the
territories of the known sins.

Okay, the only thing, maybe, was...
while my father was dying in Jersey
...and I couldn't go visit him.
No, it wasn't like I couldn't get
time off or I couldn't
afford it or the car died or nothing.
I just couldn't go.
Look at him in the bed.
Legless.
His right arm paralyzed from the strokes.
His power of speech eradicated.
Facial muscles uncontrollable.
Watch him staring at the television
all day long, screaming out the only
word his mouth could form: "Ma!"
Calling my mother.
Ma!
Whenever he needed her to turn him over.
Ma!
Or find him a Mets game on T V.
Ma!
Or turn off the harsh light.
Or put the picture of Lord Baby Jesus
just a little closer, Ma, just a
little closer, Ma! Ma! Ma.

Sorry, I couldn't watch this.
I didn't go.
For years.
I'd let my siblings deal with all
that shit while I continued to not
know and not investigate and not do
one blessed thing for the man,

outside of having fantasies of
killing him by suffocation and ending the
pretense, the Bible reading, the
and clapping, the speaking in
Tongues, the false hope, ending it,
ending it, for God's sakes let the
poor man die, why don't you?
Just let the poor man die.

Thou shall honor thy mother
and thy father.
Jesus.

ROBERT MONTANO

My wife...
...she gave her old clothes to a local church...
she knew the mailman's birthday...
she gave to UNICEF...
she sent passionate faxes to elected officials...
she knew the first
twelve Shakespeare sonnets by heart...
she said goodbye to toll booth people...
"bye-bye toll booth person!"...
she returned her library books on time...
she visited her eternal grandmother
every faithful summer...
the old woman's one remaining pleasure...
incontinent, toothless, unhappy...
connecting her granddaughter,
through endlessly repeated anecdotes,
to the history written in her blood...

...she swore she'd buy herself a gun
and shoot herself in the head
before she'd put up with an old age like this...
we planned to get ancient together
and do the joint-suicide thing...

...but there was a guy...

...a guy who washes car windows
in front of the bank in our neighborhood...
young guy...
filthy...
heroin...
always had a skateboard...
she'd drive up to the bank...
give him a dollar to clean the windshields...

...they'd hang out and talk...
they did this every Saturday morning...
he's very good-looking...
despite the filth...

...she used to shoot up, so she understood...
I thought they were in love...
they had "a thing"...
I waited in the car as they laughed...
she once gave him a twenty,
got in the car, crying...
she said, "I just heard the saddest story"...

...his new tattoo...
I swore it was her name
surrounded by a crown of thorns...
the woman he couldn't have...
I wanted to kill this man...
he was pathetic...
smelled like a urinal...
she got too close to him...
I didn't want his clothes to brush her clothes...
came home one day...
there he is *in the kitchen*...
merrily drinking coffee...
he's talking to her about movies...
big fan of Hitchcock...
what the fuck is going on here?...
I wanted to unwind...

I'm stuck with this putrid drug-user
in my kitchen
pontificating about *Strangers on a Train!*...

...we fought about it that night...
I told her: "I come home...
I can't even talk to you
because this addict is monopolizing you...
all I want is equal rights here!"...
she said,
"I already know what you're going to tell me"...
I stare at her...
"I *bore* you?...
is that it?"...
"No," she said quickly...
I didn't even stay in bed to hear more...
she said, "these people need me"...
"I don't need you?"...
she said, "not in the same way"...
"honey, I need you in profound ways"...
she said, "yes I know"...
"You're not going to save this man"...

...I couldn't stop imagining them together...
I imagined them sharing a cardboard box...
they do it on rusted mattresses...
passion heightened by rusted mattress spikes
stabbing their naked butts...
in fact, pain is the goal...

...I imagined they road skateboards together...
panhandling in front of our house...
all our friends staring at her...
and she'd look and sound happier
with him than she ever looked and sounded
with me...
beneath the layers of traffic soot
and sidewalk dirt
her eyes were full of wisdom and fulfillment

and absolute freedom...
the freedom only vaguely imagined
by the housebound...
freedom to say "fuck you"...
to stare at the drivers
waiting for the light to change...
she'd challenge them:
"Hey you in the Lexus, are you moral?
empathic?...
you think you are...
you tell your children you are...
in your prayers you boast that you are...
yet here I am...
LOOK AT ME...
I'm staring into the deepest tunnels
of your heart
and I'm not seeing shit...
you want me gone...
you hope I fall off the edge
of the known world...
fall painlessly into oblivion
while you drive to your appointments"...

...she wanted that power...
and that power was something
she could only get from him...

...then he disappeared...

...after that we would drive together...
anywhere...
didn't matter...
there they were...
like an army of vampires,
bloodless, in their rags and filth...
they knew about her...
they sought her out...
she radiated goodness and they wanted it...
they wanted to drink from her kindness

like it was an ancient tribal river...
to suck her down into their limbs...
to own her...

...my wife...
actually began to disappear in front of my eyes...
I watched helpless as she gave away
scraps of herself...
first the excess...
then the vital tissues...
until she disappeared completely from my sight...
down into the tortured piranha pit
of the homeless...

...away from me...
happy...
alive...

and finally at home.

VANESSA MARQUEZ

I caused the Northridge earthquake.
Me! How did I do it? How do I know?
Because the night of the earthquake
I was in the Northridge Hospital.
I was paralyzed from the waist down
from a car accident I got into on the 10.
I was in the hospital for months.
I wasn't improving.
I couldn't stop crying!
But the night of the earthquake,
I was lying in bed,
trying with all my heart and soul
to move my useless legs.
And you know what?
I did! I moved my legs—
and just at that very same second,

the earthquake happened!
I made the whole earth shake with my tiny legs!
Houses fell.
Mountains shifted.
Continents kissed and divorced!
Cracks went down deeper than any hell
I could imagine!
And I did that! Me.
All by myself.

And that terrified me.
And I saw what I did
to all those people and houses
and I cried and asked God to forgive me.
I just didn't know, God!
I was humbled and inspired
and now I can walk.
Now I can walk.

ANA ORTIZ

There's somebody...I don't know who he is...I want to take this time to apologize to him. I don't know your name. I don't know what you look like.

You were in the Bronx about seven years ago. Let's see, it was outside the 180th Street stop on the Two, close to one in the morning. I don't remember the name of the street anymore.

But right there, under the elevated tracks, at the intersection, on the left as you go east, one night seven years ago ... I saw you.

It was very dark there. All I wanted to do was to get home. So I'm walking fast 'cause I hate that street and I almost didn't see you. But I did see you.

Two men were holding you by the arms and they
where slamming you head-first into the front of a
parked car. I couldn't see your face. The two guys were
laughing. You fell to the ground. I only watched for a
second.

I got out of there as fast as I could. I went home. I didn't
call the cops. I didn't call for help. I didn't jump in to
break it up. I didn't go back later to see if you were
okay. I didn't do nothing but run. Protect my ass.

For a second I actually convinced myself that you guys
were playing some kind of game, maybe you were just
kids.

I'm sorry. If you're out here. If you're hearing this.
I was the one who walked away that night and left you
there and I haven't been able to stop thinking about you
in seven years and I thought, here, now, this would be
the time to say I was sorry. This would be the time.

Please forgive me, sir. Please forgive me.

CARLO ALBAN

I see some gods on the moon.
I also see it moving, just a little,
lets pretend my hand is the moon,
it's going like this.

The moon has too much light.
I think it's the gods.
They're having fires there.
The light shoots!
It goes past all the black air in space
and hits my eyes and I feel the hot too,
the hot light from the gods on the moon.
I can't hear them talking,
they're too far away.

I think they're mad at us.
I think they want to blow us up.
They talk whispering.
If we went in the clouds with machine guns
and arrows
we could kill them.
We hate them.
The gods have no eyes.
They left their eyes at home.
Their hearts are squish and their
blood is really smooth and warm.
It feels like this.

They waited a long time.
They watch us.
They know everything we do.
Some day we're all going to get real sick
and have a disease
and be really dead, everybody.
Like all the dinosaurs and pterodactyls did.
But faster.
In one night we'll all die and lie down in bed
and fall asleep and be dead.
That's when the gods on the moon
will find their eyes and come down to earth,
and take the whole place over.

JOHN VARGAS

I was obsessed with the veins in her neck!
I could see her blue thick veins
running from her chin down to her chest,
along the velvet hills of her skin,
these arteries full of rich, dark blood,
twisting around like the friggin' streets of L A.
Every time I drove I felt myself traveling the veins
of her neck, getting lost in her hot Cuban bloodstream...

But it was so stupid because
it was so fucking doomed because
even if I wasn't married to her sister,
even if I was single,
I was all wrong for her!
She's into bad boys!
Men with prison records!
Chain smokers! Tattoos!
I didn't even have facial hair!
I hated loud noises!
She liked ex-heroin addicts!
There's a certain romance to men like that!
A mystique!
There was absolutely no friggin' chance for me!
It was pathetic!
It was sickening!
I was disgusted with my life!
I went out west to fucking escape
and my fucking life decided to follow me!
I wasn't a man!

God help me,
I was a parody of a man.

SVETLANA EFREMOVA

I would breathe against the window and watch the thin
white cloud my breath made on the glass and I would
take a finger and write an X in the mist. Then I would
move ever-so-slightly left or right and I would exhale
again and make another small cloud on the glass and
again I would make an X. I did this until I had covered
the entire window in that room with the white anxious
smoke of my lungs. Then I would go to the next
window and start over and make small Xs, row upon
row, small exact Xs, engraved in the temporary surface
my breath made on the cold window panes.

I wouldn't even look outside. I never took my eyes off
the small X, then the next virgin spot on which there
wasn't an X. And even if I had wanted to look outside,
it would have been pointless to look, as the other side
of the window was inches thick with dirt and car
exhaust and pigeon shit. The light that penetrated that
window was a urine-colored little spit of light, a little
piss of light fighting the compacted air and finally
leaking into the room, yellow and anxious, like a
diabetic's piss.

There were nine windows in the room and nine is the
number of redemption.

I don't know why I made so many Xs. I was amazed
by this activity. I couldn't stop. Not even when they
brought the food. Little trays with neatly wrapped
sandwiches, which I ignored until I was nearly
starving, but ate quickly because I didn't want to stop
making Xs on those silent nine windows. In fact hunger
only heightened my desire, motivated me, gave me
a heroic reason to continue the punishment, the
shameful, secret ritual that had locked its iron jaws
around my mind.

I began to despise myself for my weakness: it wasn't a
voice, or a pair of hands, but some force had seized me
and all my cursing and rebellious fantasies were wasted
on it. Superior and inexhaustible it commanded, yes,
commanded me to continue.

Why did I obey? I loved food. I loved going to the
bathroom. I loved living in my dreams. I loved
exploring sin, but only in my imagination. Outside of
my imagination I was terrified of sin and would never
commit one and I'd follow every rule, man-made or
dictated by God, no matter how absurd, I listened,
I followed. Fear motivated me and I never strayed from
the narrow pathway leading from birth to death. I let
pleasures elude me. I let people walk away from me,

free of my fantasies of them, innocent of my deeply
buried desires and dreams, the twisting, fantastic,
highly-plotted, improbable living dreams in which I
satisfied every need and never paid for it, never lost a
lover, never felt guilt, never apologized. I turned my
back on everything in order to make little miniature X's
on the surface of great industrial windows, tightly
interconnected X-patterns as elaborate and lovely as the
Book of Kells.

What was I trying to make? What code was I trying to
break?

At times I was vaguely aware of others in the room
with me. I didn't know if they were real or ghosts. I was
aware of distant voices, detached and clinical, voices
that freeze your blood and incense your mind, voices I
tried to ignore as I covered those vast windows in Xs.
I wanted to stop and address the voices. To turn around
and viciously insult whoever it was who spoke to me
in such rude and disrespectful ways. But I found I
couldn't turn around. I couldn't stop making Xs in the
windows. Night after night, sleepless, nearly starved,
I continued my work in light that obscured my vision
and among voices that confused my hearing.

I imagined my fists breaking through the window.
I imagined throwing my only chair through the
window. I imagined great pure sunlight storming into
the room: then air: pure air! And, then, space beyond
the window, space to walk and breathe and really live.
I imagined eating food again and having lovely bowel
movements and rerunning my sexual fantasies and
getting an apartment and a car and maybe a tempt job
in a secure office, some old corporation that would take
good care of me.

I would like that. I would develop as a human being in
that scenario. I would acquire a small selection of elite
books. The great thoughts of mankind. I'd buy C Ds

and listen to the latest tunes. I would flourish within
the context of new friendships. People would bring me
news of distant places. All would find my story of the
room and the Xs appalling and fascinating. I would
develop a reputation as an appalling and fascinating
individual. No one at the corporation would suspect
the depth of the quiet and loyal little functionary in the
next cubicle. Storage of so many secrets would only
enhance my mental powers. I have been a wanderer,
an explorer of the twisting pathways of the mind.
My passport is stamped by nations grotesque and
wonderful.

Over and over again I would be aware of my moral
superiority. Over and over again...over and over
again...over and over again...as I made my Xs. As I
made my Xs in my urine-colored room I realized how
stupid these fantasies were. How abject and cruel.
My fantasies made me sick. And in that sickness I
found a strange liberation.

A strange liberation is what you gave me.

JESSICA HECHT

The air killed me.
I was sensitive—
but not any more
than the average person, I think.
I liked to breathe.

Breathing was a good thing.
I had an office on Wilshire and La Brea.
The Asahi Building, 11th floor,
a balcony that went three quarters
the way around the building,
you had a view east south and west.
Spectacular sometimes when the air was invisible.

But that was rare:
most times it clung to the ground
like mustard gas,
like some kind of white moss,
like a viral infection
along the tissues of your moist lungs—
like the kiss of death,
like a bad chance,
a freak ghost,
a haunting,
polluted Karma,
warmed over holistic spiritual bullshit.

I would stand on my balcony
trying to see vistas
and downtown structures
and only see the brown death-clouds
of our automotive suicide
and I'd stand there
coughing and cursing like a tubercular mad freak,
face all red, phlegm the color of unsanitary blood—
I could taste multinational oil giants
in the unhappy folds of my violated tastebuds;
I could taste Middle East petrodollars
in my hacking dry wheezing breath
and I'd cough and I'd curse
like some twentieth century version of Captain Ahab—
I swear I could feel one of my legs
turning into wood—
ranting against the visible air,
shaking my fist at the death clouds,
spitting at the smudged and indifferent horizon,
straining to see the so-called beauty
in the so-called mountain ranges
and my eyes slamming into that beige curtain,
that soiled atmosphere,
and I'd curse its opacity and its density;
I'd curse its weight

and its love of gravity and streetlevel;
I'd curse its vile and indefeatible smugness,
its certainty that in this minuscule dance of death
we had together it—
not I—would prevail;
it—not I—would be writing
the obituary for the morning paper.

That was a Monday morning
I had those thoughts.

I went home at six o'clock.
I sat in the eye-clogging, spirit-stomping traffic
traveling the four miles from the Asahi Building
to my home in Los Feliz
in about what seemed like
and couldn't have possibly been less than
one solid hour of nerve-crushing,
soul-spattering numbness.

I got home.
I was in my home.
I was contemplating a wide variety
of Trader Joe's frozen delights.
What will it be tonight, I asked myself.
The frozen Trader Joe's Chicken Burrito?
Or the frozen Trader Joe's Veggie Biryani?

I was staring at my freezer
contemplating another exciting night
of microwave, television, and insomnia...
when I notice a bright red smudge
out of the corner of my eye.
I turned to look at it.
It was a pane of glass in the kitchen window
reflecting light.

It was the kind of red
you only dream about
when you dream about absolutes.

The red from the inside of your corpuscles
or the center of a volcano's burning stomach
or the red of infinite anger
or the deepest passion.

I realized it was reflecting the light
coming in from the living room.
I went to the living room
and looked out the big bay windows.
The windows that face west.
The sun was going down.

How do I explain this?
The dirty air created the most—
it was the most fantastic—
no, it, it, it was the most spectacular—
no, it was an explosion of oranges and reds—
no, that doesn't do it:
that doesn't say how
fuckingly fuckingly fuckingly beautiful
that sunset was that evening
hovering like red liquid over the West,
the airdust twisting and bending
the rays of final sunlight
like the shapes in a Calder mobile,
or the ornate lines
of the Shahnama-yi Shahi,
those rays of light
were twisted and bent
beyond imaginable wavelengths
and color patterns:
I saw lava in the sky,
I saw lung tissue,
I saw rose petals,
I saw bloodied mountains,
I saw red rainbows...
and I saw it change
and undulate and tease

and I said to myself,
I gotta go outside
and get a better look at this,
I gotta have one really good experience
in this no exit day.
So I walked down the steps to the driveway
to get a better look at the sunset.

At that very exact moment
my next door neighbor Lourdes,
a woman about my age,
with a waterfall of churning black hair
and eyes like big radar dishes,
she was coming out of her apartment
to look at the pollution-created,
spectacular, massively red display of,
I don't know: pure glory.
And the both of us
just stood there long minutes
watching this sky-thing
changing and rotating
and I didn't even notice she was there
and we didn't notice each other
as the sun disappeared
and the sky darkened
and I swear I'd never seen this woman in my life
and it turns out we've been neighbors
for three years
and she lives with two roommates
and it's a little crazy
and lately the walls have been closing in
and I explained I lived alone
and my walls are closing in too
and wasn't that the most incredible looking sunset
any person has ever seen?
And isn't it funny we both decided
it was so beautiful
we had to venture outside

to get a really good look at it?
And why don't you come over
and have some
frozen Trader Joe's Calamari in Oyster Sauce with me?
And sure that would be fun.

And she came over
and we played my old Lightning Hopkins records
I haven't listened to in half a century
and she told me stories of loss and sadness
and she cried on my shoulder
and I cried on hers
and we exchanged
fleeting tender fingertip touches
and I do believe
that was the very last time
I ever cursed the air pollution in my life.

GENO SILVA

I grew up with a guy who is now
the most famous T V producer of all time.
Same neighborhood.
Same girlfriends, everything,
and that motherfucker stole the Fonze off me.
We came to Hollywood the same time.
I had an idea for a show.
I said to him two words: "the Fifties."
That's all I said!
And, before you know it,
this cocksucker's got *Happy Days* on the air!
He steals the Fonze from me!
My creation!
The voice, the leather jacket, the hair,
the look, I did the "look,"
everything, the cool control Fonzie had,
the way he could just slice through a situation

like a red hot razor blade,
the anti-hero loneliness,
the outsider metaphysic,
the cleft chin,
all of that, all of that was mine,
and the motherfucker stole it from me
and made a fucking fortune
while I found myself sitting in an office
with a Jew with plugs in his head
pitching to Hispanics!

ANTIONETTE ABBAMONTE

There were three boys.
One on each arm.
They pulled my arms back and it hurt.
I couldn't get loose.
I couldn't kick them.
They weren't very strong
but they were determined.

The third boy was in front of me
trying to dodge my kicks,
looking for an opening,
trying to get a good solid punch in
and I kept fighting
and a couple of other boys
were starting to gather
and laugh
and nobody went to get a teacher
or a parent
and when the boy in front of me
finally saw his opening
he punched me right in the chest
and I felt my head exploding
as if all the blood from his punch
was rushing right up into my face.

I could feel my mouth opening
and saliva coming out of it
and the laughter was even stronger
after that
and I looked up at the school
and I could see a couple of girls
looking down at me
from the second floor window
and they weren't moving or anything,
I think one of them was shaking her head no,
but no one was rushing down
to save me
and that's when I understood
the depth of the conspiracy against me,
and I started to laugh,
and the next time I looked up
at the second floor of the school,
I could see myself
looking down at myself,
not moving,
like I was another co-conspirator,
maybe even the worst one,
maybe the leader,
looking down at myself,
passive,
holding hands with the cold girls at my side,
just slowly, slowly shaking my head no.

KARENJUNE SANCHEZ

I'm sorry.
I'm just a little freaked out at the moment.
I thought I was going somewhere else.
I thought—
because my father was black

and my mother was Hawaiian—
I'd be going somewhere else.

I'm twenty-eight.
I was born and raised in El Paso.
My father was the king of hardware and lumber.

There was a hole in the floor next to the bed.
It was very black.
My mother and father were still very poor—
before Pop became king of hardware and lumber.
We moved into this little house on the West Side.
We weren't there long.
In any case, my father filled that hole
the next day.
But my first night in that house,
I slept in a bed next to that hole in the floor
that was black and deep and quiet.

The first one to climb out of that hole
in the floor called himself Ace Man.
He was a card player from San Antonio
who died in a car accident
the day he quit his job for Bekins
and was speeding through Oklahoma
to see a new girlfriend—
a woman whose furniture he moved himself.
Ace Man had long ears and a tiny mustache
and was half Mexican, half Hopi.
I was eight years old and we played cards
for hours and he always beat me.

He cried out loud for his lost love
and how he never got to live with her
and how unfair it is to get killed
the day your freedom arrives
and you're on the road
and the radio's playing *Free Bird*
and the earth seems endless
and the people in it seem slightly less evil.

His friends eventually came out of the hole too:
they had funny names like
Little Finger and Clay and Smokes and Chieftain and
Lagrimas and Sparky
and all of them were mixed bloods
of some kind or another
and coming from different
and conflicting cultures
they didn't know what afterlife to go to
so they hung around this narrow hole in El Paso
for the rest of time
and they all had tales of loss and regret
and told jokes
because the loss and regrets didn't get them down
and they knew how to party
and forget their pain,
and they gave me advice
on how to live in the world
and be myself
and fight my fights,
and see the unusual in the usual,
and turn darkness into light and laughter,
and even with tears in their eyes
they knew how to laugh,
and sometimes the saddest ones
laughed the loudest,
and I thanked those imperfect souls
and I kissed each one goodnight
and each one slipped back
into the hole in the floor
and the next day my father
covered it up forever with cement.

And that's where I always thought I'd end up:
in a covered-up hole in a bedroom floor
in El Paso, Texas.

YUSEF BULOS

Three days in the city.

Day One. I'm walking up Hollywood Blvd. with my
son. We're taking pictures of the stars on the sidewalk.
Trying not to stare at the people. A man with a hat
made of television parts. Homeless women picking
scabs. Teenagers so thin they disappear like the
sideways view of the rings of Saturn. Scientologists in
neat blue uniforms walking briskly to their nautical
salvation. In Dayton you just don't see these variations.
A couple of limos whispering past us. A few times I
thought I recognized someone from something. Day
One in the city.

We stop at a big candy store. My son has died and
gone to heaven. He buys little packets of false tattoos.
Kids wear them all the time. I'm dreading what forms
of brilliant rebellion he'll be into by the time he's a
teenager. He puts a little *Jurassic Park* tattoo on his arm
and begs me to put a tattoo on my arm. I didn't want to.
Felt silly, of course.

But this was the first time in six months that he and I
had spent an entire day together. Every second of the
day was just him and me. Asks me a million "why"
questions, it's that phase. I can see more of myself in
him than ever before. Recognize my own reactions.

It wasn't always like this. I resented his birth. It was
unexpected, unplanned. I went into a nose-dive.
I fretted about money so obsessively I went into
counseling. I fought with my wife. I hated waking
up each morning. I looked longingly at younger
unattached women and dreamed of unattachment.
I would hold my newborn son and feel nothing. His

crying grated on me. I had recurring fantasies in which I ran away and was never heard from again.

Then one night, it was two or three in the morning, and his crying woke me up and I told my wife I would give him a bottle. The house was silent. Only one light burned near us. I was barely awake. I held my son in the living room—it was only a few seconds before that miracle happened—and it was suddenly as if I had just awakened from a deep and troubling sleep—and I was instantly aware that I had a son.

A son.

I was looking at him as if I had never seen him before and in that second, I remember it so vividly even now, in that second I remember falling deeply in love with him—it was the first and only time in my entire life that I actually experienced the "fall" of falling in love—a swift endless drop, wind blowing in my face, down a perfectly delicious abyss...and I just...I couldn't control myself...I held him...and cried with him and I didn't want to let go. Not ever. Not for another second of my life.

Anyway. There we were on Hollywood Blvd. In this labyrinthine candy store and he wants me to put this scorpion tattoo on my arm. Finally, I relent. I apply the temporary tattoo to my forearm. A big green scorpion, vivid and nasty: it looks very convincing.

We walk out onto the boulevard, looking into absurd little lingerie stores, trying to explain to this little boy what that's for, trying not to stand out in general.

Suddenly a couple of young men approach us. Hispanic boys. They're very young and their heads are shaven and they wear long baggy white T-shirts, baggy pants: chocolate complexions, dark eyes, good-looking boys, but hardened, their mouths were set in this frown, it looked permanent, as if they could easily break out in tears any second—and I rapidly tried to imagine their fathers—you know how the mind works—what do their fathers do, what do they think of these strong-looking young men with the permanently sad faces—I know their fathers must have experienced the fall I experienced with my son—so how could they possibly let these vulnerable little boys out of their sight?—how could we have gotten to this moment of confrontation and implied violence?—and they're looking at me very hard and they point to the child's tattoo of the scorpion on my arm and say something very quietly to me in Spanish. I don't understand what it is. Then one of them points to his forearm—he has the tattoo of a spider on his arm. And I don't understand any of this and my radar is going, "get the hell out of there: get out now"—and I try to move on, and they won't let me go on and my son's crying and finally the shorter of the two looks at my son and notices his *Jurassic Park* tattoo and realizes my scorpion is just a toy and not a real tattoo and I'm not in some rival gang, like who could believe that?—the Dayton white guy gang?—and this young man laughs so hard and loud—laughs with relief—I laugh too—and he says, "que vida mas loca"—"sorry, mister; whatta crazy life," in lilting, accented English and moves on.

Day Two—imagine my surprise: I'm crossing a street in Beverly Hills, don't watch my step because I'm eyeing an extraordinary blonde in a top they would have prosecuted her in Dayton for, and a limo plows right into me at top speed, sending me to the intensive care unit at Cedar Sinai Hospital.

Day Three and here I am.

Can you tell me how to get word to my son, please? I want to tell him not to worry about me.

FELICITY JONES

They think I lied. I didn't lie! I had an active
imagination but I didn't lie about this. It was a brain
tumor! Jesus Christ!

The deadline had come and gone. I had finished the
script, I really had. But it still didn't work. It needed
tweaking. I told them down at Universal that it was
almost ready. Give me a couple of weeks to tweak the
stupid thing.

It was a genre picture. I had never done a genre picture
before. New rules I had to learn. Very strict ones. Movie
haiku. I held my breath and went for it. Stretched
myself.

I always take my time. I'm slow. Sue me but everyone
in the business knows that going into it and if you can't
deal with it, don't fucking hire me!

So I missed the deadline. No one panics. Not yet. We
agree on another deadline. That one comes and goes.
Tempers under control, okay good. Another deadline.
My manager is now starting to crack at the seams.
Pieces of him are starting to fall off. The Universal
people are getting ugly.

Look, I had a reputation for being excellent at my craft.
Then I finished the thing and started having a brain
tumor.

I called the studio. The script is close I said but I can't
finish it because I have a brain tumor. They thought I
lied. I didn't lie! I didn't! I could feel it throbbing in my
cranium. It was like I was having a baby in my head.
Like Athena was pounding the inside of my face with
her big Bronze Age spear and this tumor started
assuming shapes.

The shapes of an ex-husband. Screaming at me for
being lazy and indecisive. Leaving me for a younger,
happier version of myself. It was taking on the shape
of famous people. Joan of Arc was being burned at an
imaginary stake in my mind every night. I could hear
the fire in my sleep. I could smell the smoke. The doctor
said phantom smells were the first sign of a brain
tumor. But it was the screaming that convinced me.

It wasn't my screaming. It was the screaming of the
brain tumor that had assumed the shape of Sharon Tate
in my brain, this blob of extra-busy brain cells that
multiplied and conquered and assumed the shape of
famous victims.

I had the operation. They took the tumor out of my
head. I finished the script and the studio made the
movie and I was nominated for my third Academy
Award. Awesome dress.

I kept the tumor. I kept it in my house. It's in the
refrigerator in a Tupperware-like container. It's now
in the shape of, well, oddly enough, me. It's a little
miniature me that I talked to and got advice from and
all the neighbors and agents in town and actors who
owed their careers to me thought I was crazy. But I
wasn't. I didn't lie.

My tumor got on the phone and lied for me.

DORIS DIFARNECIO

I heard the truck's engine.
It was loud.
But not as loud as the wind.

A tornado wind!
I was in the back of the truck.
I was wearing Papa's old army jacket,

big and soft, smelled like him,
the sweat from his travel,
the sweat from his work,
picking oranges and artichokes.
His jacket was alive with memories
of his labors and the sweat mixed in
with the sugar and tears of all those places.
The place by the tracks,
by the slaughterhouse,
at the edge of town:
places where nobody else would live.

We crossed a lot of borders in a truck.
Since before I was born.
Following the seasons,
the rhythms of vegetables, our masters;
little plants told us where to live and when,
and Papa listened and obeyed
and kept his mouth shut
and kept out of sight
and kept listening to the orders of the crops
and we traveled to their places
and did the work we had to do
to keep them alive
and keep America fed
and we obeyed the laws,
all the laws, we had to be careful.

And the truck was full of people that night:
a few strangers we didn't know,
also migrants, also going north.

Papa stopped for them:
I don't know why:
he never does that.

They all got into the truck with me
and Mama and Papa
and we drove north
and then the police followed us.

Papa wouldn't stop.
Maybe the strangers in the truck were afraid.
They must have told him not to stop,
to go faster, and maybe he didn't want
to look weak in their eyes
and we went faster, faster,
and the wind was louder and colder
and the truck's engine was faint,
like it had left me behind...
and I was flying through the night air,
flying like a man-eating spirit,
flying with the demons and unlucky ghosts
of the freeway...
and the police wouldn't go away;
they pushed Papa faster...
and Papa tried a U-turn...
and I remember flying into a storm.

When the storm ended,
my Mama and Papa were gone.
The storm had turned my family to rain.
And the rain fell to the earth.
They disappeared in the thirsty earth
so they could feed the plants
who ruled their lives. Gone.

KEVIN JACKSON

I was looking down at the ocean. I was nervous. The
ocean didn't frighten me. It was the sharp shooters.
They patrolled the beach every half hour. Through the
walls of the prison they could be heard telling obscene
jokes. Sometimes they were so bored they would take
target practice on the seagulls. They'd spend their
entire complement of arrows on the seabirds.

No, the ocean didn't frighten me. I loved heights—my
love grew stronger as the years of incarceration went

by. Everything was far, far below us. The enemies who imprisoned us seemed no larger than ticks.

Our prison was the tallest structure in the country. You could see it from a hundred miles away. And everyone knew that my father and I, the most wanted criminals in the country, were trapped there, finally outsmarted, the genius and his only son contained in stone and steal, a prison even his great mind couldn't outwit. Or so they thought. My father, of course, had other plans.

At first he wouldn't even trust me with his scheme. Afraid, maybe, I'd break under torture and spill my guts. In the morning he'd draw elaborate diagrams. Study them all day. Then destroy them every night for fear the guards would find them during their periodic raids of his cell.

After a year in prison my father started asking the guards for extra candles. He was an avid reader and his eyes were going. The guards, rightfully suspicious, didn't pay him any attention. Then he went on a hunger strike—his tenth, I believe—and threatened to somehow contact the human rights groups monitoring our imprisonment—and this always freaked out the powers-that-be, and after nearly six months of strikes, near-deaths, stalemates, and plain old fashioned hardball, my father got what he wanted. Two extra candles every night. I knew, instantly, that a plan was in effect.

But he was subtle. He let another six months pass.

Then my father started to complain that his shit was bloody. He requested that his diet be supplemented with grains. A month passed before he got what he wanted. A handful of grain. Then things started to pick up.

My father would put the grain on the high ledge of his one window. Inevitably a seabird would land and eat the grains. The opening was small and my father would frighten the birds so suddenly they would flap their wings while still on the ledge and inevitably the wild beating of wings against the stone window would shake feathers loose and the feathers would fall to the floor in my father's cell. This happened every day.

And it was this way, slowly, that my father collected his treasure of white feathers.

And he would melt his wax from his two extra candles and glue those feathers together and in a year's time he had fashioned identical pairs of giant wings. Then we fasted until we each weighed less than a hundred pounds.

The day came. I was looking down at the ocean. I was nervous. The ocean didn't frighten me. It was the sharpshooters. They were on the beach that day. And, again, bored and stupid, they were wasting their arrows on the hapless seabirds. When the tall one shot his very last arrow into the air, my father said, "come on."

Through a hole in the wall my father had patiently carved out of solid rock during the years of our incarceration, we barely squeezed ourselves and our mighty wings.

As he predicted the wind was northerly. For years he had watched the patterns of the clouds, making mental notes, filed away in the great cavern of that magnificent brain, and understood the rhythms of the air, of temperature, of clouds—and predicted this day would be cloudless, no rain, no lightning, no turbulence.

We had to move fast. We climbed through the hole. We were outside for the first time in years. We strapped on our wings. The sharpshooters saw us. The fools started to shout commands! They started throwing rocks but of course the tower was much higher than any man can

throw and seconds after attaching the wings to our
bodies, we were lifted by a current of air.
When my feet left the ground, I gasped! I had never
known such a feeling! I started to involuntarily kick the
air, as if that would help me fly higher and faster, but it
only dragged me down and my father told me to knock
it off. "It's all in the arms," he said and he demonstrated
and was instantly high above me, flying homeward, as
if he had been born to it.

I was astonished! And the energy of my astonishment
was the power I used to lift myself above the prison
tower, even as an army of sharpshooters arrived on the
beach with their arsenal of crossbows.

Now at this point in the story I have to stop to correct a
misconception. It is believed by many people that it was
arrogance and pride that attracted me to the sun that
day and resulted in my downfall.

No. It was not. It was something altogether different
that brought me down.

The reason I faltered is this: I was sick of my father's
perfection.

I knew I carried his genes in me, knew my tendency to
lose my temper, as well as my weak left eye and my
natural suspiciousness all came from him. But the
greater gifts, the gifts of the mind, those he hoarded
and kept in the dark locked tower of his superior I Q.
And every day I tried to match him, I showed him my
drawings, my escape plans, my elaborate and fanciful
weapons—and every time he'd laugh at me, point out
the obvious flaw in each of them, tell me not to bother
myself because the strain would be too much for my
inferior intellect and of course he was hatching a
foolproof scheme. He'd smile at me, a condescending
smile, the smile an animal trainer gives to his clever and

limited chimpanzee, the smile I had to endure my entire life long.

I had a right to think myself superior to him! My legs were longer, my eyes clearer, my endurance greater—but I didn't think myself superior.

That tower was cold, always cold. As we flew upward into the blue air above the ocean, I flew straight for the sun. I flew toward what was warm—away from the cold father whose own heart was buried deep within its private labyrinth, inaccessible to all.

Yes, I wanted to show him his invention was flawed and I knew what that flaw was! I could hear him yelling: "You idiot! You fly too high! Don't fly so high!" "Why not?" I shouted back. "The wings! The wax will melt! You'll ruin the wings!"

That's my story.

I tell it to everyone. I'm telling it to you. You don't have to believe me. I suppose, in this space, you have to tell the truth. I'm telling the truth. That's the story of my father and me, before I came to New York.

The wax melted, I fell out of the sky, I crashed into the ocean, I was rescued by fishermen off the coast of Maine, in a coma. I came to, I begged my doctors to go out to sea and find the remains of my beautiful wings. I was pleasantly and firmly rehabilitated.

I pretended to forget my childhood and my brilliant father and my one incredible flight over the sea. But I won't forget.

I cleave to my story, imagining that somewhere nearby my father has again escaped death and is again laughing brilliantly at all of us.

X

Mixed blood is shit.

You're just fuckin' crazy, lady.

Black man with a story about flying! Shit!

Bring it, bitch! Here I am!

I fucked people up.
Blood was like food to me.
Like a God of the night.
Killed a man in the Bronx seven years ago.
Smashed his face clean into the grill of a Lincoln
Continental with whitewalls,
leather interior, nice shine.
You think I'm sorry?
I'd do it again.
You think I'm afraid?
Don't none of you think I'm going to change.

MARK FERREIRA

This body is a book.
And in my head I can hear
the voices of ancestors:
they've already spoken richly to my genes.
Left their ironies and paradoxes imprinted there.
The voices of my ancestors are nightmare voices,
insistent, untranslatable.
They want me to remember
what part of my body came from the Caribbean.
What part came from Africa. Spain.
The Canary Islands.

They ask me: when a nation fights a war are those
battles imprinted on the D N A of the survivors?
What screams are encoded there?
Battle plans, moments of heroism,
a young soldier pissing his pants...
which moments become part of the collective memory
to be translated into proteins,
effecting the shape of organs,
thickness of marrow,
location of heart valves,
brain circuits,
patterns of sleep?
What does peace mean in this context?
Don't we tear holes in the wind itself
when we make war?

These are my talkative ghosts:
manifestations of the past,
acting out old patterns,
tugging on living flesh,
inept and weak, but there, very
there, very right now.
History acts on us like big magnets,
like time's finger tips.
A slave's impulses, a leader's perspiration,
a buried son, the color of a flag—
nothing is wasted.
Everything is recycled.

I ask my ancestors:
Who had my face before?
Who shaped my brain?
They laugh.
They know I carry my nation's tragedies with me.
I sing its anthems.
Its coastline mirrors the shape of my back.
I know the laughter and faces of my people
are encoded forever in my deep spaces.

CORDELIA GONZALEZ

On my back, *carajo*, exhausted, couldn't even smoke one
fucking cigarette, *esse maricon* doctor and his stupid
rules. The baby in the nursery, *gracias a Dios*; I didn't
wanna see him. *Dejame quieta*, I know he's my son but,
puneta, tu sabes, at that moment, flat on my back, *carajo*,
I was grateful for a little rest, maybe watch T V, catch a
soap, though it hadda be an American soap, *Days of Our
Fucking Lives*, couldn't expect those fucking white boys
to let me watch *una telenovela, coño*.

I didn't feel too bad. My fucking body. I could give
birth in my sleep, *carajo*. I could have a baby through
my nose! I was so good at having *niños*, fuck me,
I really couldn't hardly feel him being born. Sixteen
friggin' children! *Coño!* And no twins! You try it!
That's gotta be a world's record! Somebody gotta
look that up in a book or something. Get me a door
prize of some kind! Sixteen little motherfuckers!

No, I love them, I do, I love every fucking hair on
their little fucking heads. Some of my girls, bless them,
they saved my life, *Dios mio*. They do a lotta work.

Now another baby! My body! I look like a
hippopotamus! My skin don't even feel like skin
no more.

So where is he? *Donde esta esse maricon?* Not here, at his
wife's side, not next to the mother of his sixteen little
people, holding her hand, bringing her ice cubes and
shit! Just like him, Fernando always found an excuse
to miss the birth of his babies. Sixteen kids and he ain't
never seen one of the little motherfuckers being born,
carajo. Que barbaridad!

So the baby was sleeping. I was resting. My husband was missing in action. And I'm mellow and the phone rang. I said "what?" No answer. I said, "who the fuck is this already?" *Coño!*

So then she answers. She only says one thing, one sentence. "Well," she says, "you had his baby last night, but I fucked him." Click!

Man, I slammed that fucking telephone so hard! I almost broke my fucking hand! That bitch! That cheap fucking *hija de la puneta! Me cago en tu madre!* She called me to tell me that. "You had his baby last night but I fucked him." *Mira que cosa mas* fucked up! That's where that *maricon* was last night. With his girlfriend and she calls me to tell me about it! What a class act, huh? *Coño!*

The day passed okay after that. After I settled down.

Then the phone rang again. It was my daughter Lizbeth, the oldest, she's all hysterical, I can't understand her—"*que te pasa, muchacha? Que te pasa?*" She can't settle down and passes the phone to Julian, my oldest boy, *y Julian esta llorando tambien. Ahora me pongo nerviosa.* "*Que paso, carajo,* what's up with you?" *Julian me dice,* "*Papi's* been hit by a car, *Mami.*"

I don't breathe for a minute. I don't even think.

Julian goes, "he was walking from a friend's house." A friend! From that bitch's house, *essa demonia!* "*Tu Papa se murio?*" I ask. "No. But they think he's gonna be paralyzed, Mami." "Paralyzed where?" I ask. "Paralyzed from the waist down," he says. Fernando paralyzed from the waist down....

Julian can't talk. He was crying too hard. Surprise. I thought Julian hated his father. Fernando was ruthless with his children and he gave his worst punishments to Lizbeth and Julian. Maybe they were crying from happiness.

KRISTINE NIELSEN

I always came out Wednesday night
to drop my garbage on the curb.
I lived in a quiet neighborhood,
mixed, you know? Basic Seattle.

Neighbors where Chinese—a doctor
and his wife, a guidance counselor.
Two children.

The wife—
she was a very polite woman, very civil.
She wasn't very tall.
She had small shoulders.
Her hair was short and she had a quick, gasping laugh
that made her sound startled and alert.

I didn't know a lot about psychiatry.
Or how the mind works.
I didn't dream much.
But I studied sounds.

Sounds were my source of knowledge of people.
Especially laughs.
I could gauge intelligence levels from a good laugh.
I could analyze prejudices, weaknesses, fears, desires,
from any kind of laugh,
from any kind of person.

God, if you laughed, I could tell you a little about
yourself.
Tell you what kind of day you're having.

God's not laughing today.

Anyway, her laugh was a rich tapestry for me.
I heard her anxieties in her laughter.

I heard the years of stress.
I heard her husband's coldness
and the iron grip he had on her fate.
I heard her disappointments—
the petty racist remarks she'd hear
nearly each day at school where she worked.
I heard her lamentations in her laugh:
the job is too hard,
she's afraid her children will change,
the neighborhood is getting worse—
this and more were in the sixteenth notes
of her laughter,
the fractured melodies I heard
as clear as symphonies
from the open door of my bedroom,
far from hers,
across the street:
whole light-years and a lifetime away.

ALENE DAWSON

My son had his first day of public school Monday.
We had him in a private school in Van Nuys
but it was a little too far away for us,
too expensive, and he'd come home all sad,
saying, "how come there are no
brown faces in my school, Mom?"
So we finally got him into a magnet in Echo Park
—prestigious—
and there was an assembly Monday
and on the stage the principal got up
to talk to the new students and said,
"Okay kids, now don't you be bringing in
no guns to school in your backpacks!
Hear that, children?
I want no guns, no knives,

no chains in your lockers
or in your backpacks
or on your person."
This is the principal!
This is a magnet school in the humanities!
And she says,
"Stay close to the school,
don't wander away from campus.
There have been drive-bys in this area
so don't leave the school grounds!"
I'm thinking, oh my God!
It's getting out of control.
We're at war.
Citizens killing citizens.
We don't need the government to bomb the city.
We do it to ourselves,
taking the knife to cut open the throats
of our own children,
and then when we're out of hand,
when we're too good at that,
the police are brought in,
like an occupying army, you know,
jackboots all polished up,
hardware all glistening,
big robocop shoulders,
nightsticks ripping open the heads
of our little boys—it makes me crazy.
'Cause you know, it's all their fault!
The economy bad?
It's the black kids!
Air pollution?
The black kids did it!
The dollar down against the yen?
You know who to blame! God!
Made me want to take a rock
and hurl it at some politician,
some bozo running for Mayor,

any of those quicktongued hypocrites
assigned to protect the citizens,
'cause, no, I didn't feel protected,
I felt *exposed*, all opened up,
like some criminal was pointing
his Saturday Night Special at me
and every day I sensed those trigger fingers
out there and I was at the end
of their sights and they were just watching me,
waiting for the right splitsecond
to send a little ounce of screaming steel
into the back of my brain!
God! God! It was not to be believed!
Being a woman in this city,
sometimes, oh my God,
I needed some help!
Especially when my boy went
out that door, you know?
And my imagination has created his killer,
some sweating over-anxious rookie cop,
too afraid to piss straight,
slamming into my child at the wrong time,
in the wrong place, 'cause he's thinking,
"of course, boy's in a gang, it's natural,
they run in packs,
those boys up to no good, you bet.
But what'd you expect?
It's a genetic thing with the black kids,
they're innately less intelligent,
but don't talk to me,
it's already *proven*,
there are *statistics*,
it's testable,
they're naturally more comfortable
with a forty-five in their hands
than a volume of Faulkner."
So why the hell not cut the school budget?

Why not send them off
to some genocidal death in the penitentiary?
It's a waste of good American tax money
trying to educate these
unteachable black kids!
Jesus Christ! It's time to build
another super-prison,
you know, with a hundred nautilus machines
and hot tubs and libraries,
'cause, let's face it,
it's a whole lot nicer on the inside
than the corner of Florence and Normandie.
Going to jail is a good career move!
Oh God! If I wasn't a peaceful woman
I would've throw rocks!

Trouble is, I don't think enough people
believe in the multiplicity of God.
Not enough people understand
God's great face has a nose
and eyes of a thousand shapes and sizes
and all of us, down to the last ugliest
and lowest person, we are all the living,
walking *text* of God.
Yes, the life story of God is
written into each one of us:
we are the pages in the book of God's mind.
And if we'd just take the time
we'd be able to read God
in each other's faces,
read the funny lines as well as the lines
of wisdom and healing—
because the Word of God
isn't written in the Bible, no,
the Word of God is written in your mirror
and on your brother's black face
and in your son's blue eyes.

My son. He's the sweetest thing...
actually he's a royal pain in the ass
ninety-five percent of the time...
but for five sweet percents,
he's my angel of laughter and hope.
My mother is from Guyana.
I was trying to teach my son
a little bit about that heritage,
but it was hard, you know,
that culture's so deep
and I didn't know anything about it.
I told him about South Africa
but, you know, what's that mean?
It's not like the Lakers!
The Lakers you can get up for in the morning!
No, my son's not into Guyana or South Africa.
He's into being a boy.

RENE RIVERA

Bueno, I never really made it big as an actor. I'm not
ashamed to say that. I worked.

The damn business. Competition killed me. My skin
color, my accent, my attitude, my pride.

I could play a great drug addict. Watching myself in
dailies, I fucking scared myself.

I mugged, I stabbed, I cheated on women who trusted
me, I sold drugs to sixth grade inner city youth. All for
N B C.

A line here, five lines there, bit parts, a day player.

Gangsters, hoodlums, angry spiks, pointy black shoes.
Drunks, losers, punks, washed up dreamers, casualties,
broken, futureless, fractured men, always dangerous.
Men you couldn't trust.

I played a dozen rapists with names like Miguel, Angel,
Pedro, Jose, Juan, Miguel—did I say Miguel? In one
picture alone, I raped my best friend's wife, my
daughter (twice), a little girl who lived in the building,
white women of every kind.

On primetime, I delivered pizza, I delivered packages
in Manhattan, I snaked clogged toilets, I was a
handyman, a mechanic, a grape picker, every kind
of janitor in every kind of building, a super super,
a petty drug pusher, a drug kingpin—I've been stabbed
in the heart, tortured, poisoned, raped by convicts,
overdosed eleven times, killed in the electric chair,
hit by a subway train, eaten alive by ghetto rats,
shot by the cops so often I lost count. I hung myself.

In war pictures I was always the coward. In prison
pictures I was always the traitor who ratted on his
buddies. In westerns I was the illiterate cook the
Indians scalped in the first reel. I've been a buffoon,
an asshole, a scapegoat, a pretender, a liar, a misfit.
Children and women cheered when I died. Strangers
on the street spit at me. And what great dialogue I had:
"Take that bitch!" And "I don't care if you kill me,
Sarge, 'cause I'm going straight to hell anyway!" And
"Taste my blade, *cabron*!" Eat your heart out, Lorca!

In horror pictures, I was the asshole who walked into
the dark room when the whole audience was going:
"Don't go in there, asshole!"

I had eleven agents. Fourteen managers. Countless
addresses. I was an angry young actor, then I
swallowed anger, tried to mellow out, work with the
system, I turned down nothing, I kissed so many asses,
I walked the walk, worked out, stopped smoking,
laid off the nose candy, went to the right places, shook
hands, always looked sharp any time of the day or
night, worked on my teeth, got my tattoos burned off,
left my attitude, *mira*, at the door, made follow-up calls,

wrote notes thanking racist morons for treating me like
a bag of cum. I turned anger into ambition. I watched
young studs doing roles I would never get.

Then I got sick.

Now understand me. I was a middle-aged Latino actor.
I was married very young. I had two daughters and
their mother couldn't stand my guts and she took the
two girls away and moved to Mexico. I said, the hell
with it, and went out west. Concentrated on the
subtleties of playing junkies. I had a fantastic body
and once or twice, in the beginning, they called me
in to read for Latin stud roles, usually pimps, but twice
a male prostitute, a gigolo.

So you understand—I'm in town—separated from the
mother of my girls—I'm the Latin stud prospect of the
moment—I'm free to sleep with whoever I want—but
I can't come out. I come out to nobody. Nobody in the
business.

I go where I had to go. I do what I have to do. I don't
live with nobody for a long time. I get a fake girlfriend
for a little while. I have sex in secret. Nobody knows.

But I get sick anyway. I get it. I fight knowing it, but I
get it. And I don't tell nobody.

I get safer. I meet a man. I fall in love. We're
"roommates" now. He's decent and pure and a lot
younger than me and I tell him, "babe, you're taking
some chances" and he's the home I never had, the
island where I find some peace, the wall that surrounds
and protects me.

But, you know, I used to drink a lot. And my liver is
like melted dogshit. It's a major casualty now that I'm
bad sick.

Then I meet a young Latino writer, up and coming, he's
all skinny so I nickname him Flaco and this young man

casts me in a role that's like a Latino King Lear, big, the man is big, big appetite, big balls, big language, evil but funny! I never had a part like this and I had told myself, "no plays; I'm only concentrating on the film and T V, and no going out of town!" But this role is the real thing and I say, "screw it, I'm taking this sucker by the balls and I'm going to be great and show those racist morons what I can really do!"

And I do the play out of town and Flaco and me, we become friends. He gives me hope. He never knows the truth about me but I'm getting sicker and sicker. My liver, my blood.

I disappear from sight for a year and a half: Flaco doesn't know a thing. I make sure nobody knows.

But one day everything falls apart and I'm in the hospital and suddenly the word is on the street: "Rene's got it. Rene's sick bad." And I'm in a crappy-ass hospital in Hollywood 'cause I'm broke. I didn't want anyone to visit me but they visit and eventually even Flaco visits me towards the end, when I'm bad, really bad and people are getting emergency phone calls saying, "You better see Rene now because you may never see him again."

And one night I'm barely conscious and Flaco comes to visit me. And I know he's there even though I can't talk or open my eyes. My roommate is there and he's trying to make me laugh. He's stroking my face, going, "I know you can hear me Rene. I know you want to smile. Give me a smile, Rene, come on, I know you can do it, *corazoncito*." And I smile.

And Flaco's standing there trying to talk to me and I don't want him to see me like this. I want him to remember like I was in his play, big, big appetite, big language, evil but funny.

Then one of those pathetic excuses for a doctor comes
in and realizes I'm not getting any nourishment because
the tube they got running from my arm down to my
heart is collapsed and he's got to pull it out again and
reinsert a new tube that's not collapsed. So he pulls
it out and he's sitting at my bedside and I'm totally
unconscious and Flaco is there watching all this and the
doctor is trying to insert a new tube in my veins. And
the doctor can't get the tube back in my vein again and
I'm bleeding all over the place and I can hear that Flaco
and my roommate have stopped talking and I know
they're just watching this and the doctor is making his
pathetic excuses to Flaco and my roommate and finally
I'm so damn mad, I try to use all my strength to make
a fist and I try to punch the doctor in the face and I'm
grimacing and everything in my body wants to hurt
this man and I can make my arm move and I take a shot
at him and my fist is shaking like the D Ts and he's still
making his excuses and I try three times to hit him and
he tells Flaco he can't get this tube inside me if I keep
trying to punch him like this and asks Flaco to hold me
down, and I'm so damn mad, and Flaco grabs my left
hand and holds it down and I'm struggling against him
and my mind is going, "let me go, let me hit him, let me
keep some dignity, what are you doing here anyway,
this isn't for you, I'm not a damn show, why don't all
of you just leave me alone?" and another voice in my
brain is going, "don't get no blood on you, that damn
doctor's got twenty layers of plastic but you don't have
nothing, let go of me before I bleed on you."

I'm so weak Flaco pushes my arm down so easy.

He's close to my ear and I can hear him breathing.
His hands are strong. It's incredible to feel strong skin
again, alive blood, a feverless body, strong, I'm nothing
against that strength and I almost have to laugh the
idea of me punching the doctor, I almost have to laugh.

KIERSTEN VAN HORNE

The first time someone else's tongue enters your mouth.

The first time a child trusts you to carry them to the next room.

The first time you drive safely from Westfield, Massachusetts to San Diego with someone you're in love with.

The first time you watch birth.

The first lines of *Paradise Lost*.

The first time you make a decisive three point shot in a game that really counts.

The first time you get the dog to shit outside.

The first time you can read "I love you" in a lover's eyes.

The first time you sleep in after fucking all night long.

The first family reunion without homicidal fantasies.

The first love letter.

The first serious talk about love with your child.

The first time you contemplate suicide and change your mind.

The first hangover.

The first arrest.

The first acquittal.

The first epiphany.

The first time you hear Lorca in Spanish.

The first real friendship with a person of another race.

The first gray hair.

The first time you see Picasso's *Guernica*.

The first time you visit your birthplace.

The first time you hear Lightning Hopkins.

The first visible comet.

The first time you feel attractive and someone calls you "angel."

The first experience with something remotely like a God.

The first recovery after a serious illness.

The first beer with your father.

The first time therapy makes sense.

The first birthday of your first born.

The first time you can't walk and your lover carries you to the next room.

The first foul ball you catch in Fenway Park.

The first time you stand alone and you're scared to death and you don't change your position.

The first time you're convinced of your mortality and you laugh.

The first sunrise after the first death of a parent.

The first time you forgive the unforgivable.

The first time you see the earth from space.

The first time it is truly obvious that it was better that you had lived, at this time, in this world.

The first time you decide every moment of your life should be a work of art.

The first time you die and you breathe again and you speak to the living.

The first time you realize that it all just might have been okay.

(The people in the space look up at the silent sky around them.)

(They wait.)

(No revelations come to them. No answers. No giant bolts of lighting.)

(Just a slow fade to black)

END OF PLAY